MOROCCO, ALGERIA, TUNISIA, AND LIBYA

A FIRST BOOK
BY DON LAWSON

MOROCCO, ALGERIA, TUNISIA, AND LIBYA

FRANKLIN WATTS
NEW YORK • LONDON • 1978

Cover design by Jackie Schuman

Photographs courtesy of:
United Nations: pp. 11, 14, 24, 36, 42, 57; UN/
Food and Agriculture Organization: pp. 21, 39;
Tass from Sovfoto: p. 27; Arab Information Cen-
ter: p. 50.

Maps by Vantage Art, Inc.

Library of Congress Cataloging in Publication Data

Lawson, Don.
    Morocco, Algeria, Tunisia, and Libya.

    (A First book)
    Bibliography: p.
    Includes index.
    SUMMARY: An introduction to the history,
geography, economy, culture, and people of the
four north African countries formerly known as
the Barbary States.
    1. Africa, North—Juvenile literature. [1.
Africa, North] I. Title.
DT185.L39   961'.03   78-17770
ISBN 0-531-02233-1

CONTENTS

AFRICA'S FOUR BARBARY COAST NATIONS

Africa is the second largest continent in the world. Only Asia is larger. Europeans once spoke of it as "darkest Africa" because so little was known about this rich and varied land. In time, European exploration was followed by colonization, and gradually most of Africa fell under European control.

Colonial empires reached their height during the late 1800s. But with the turn of the century, many Africans began to demand their independence and self-government. These demands eventually resulted in the breakup of the large European empires after World War II. Today so many African nations have gained their independence that the continent is now often called "the awakening giant."

Among those African nations that have gained their independence since the end of World War II are Algeria, Libya, Morocco, and Tunisia. Before the war, Libya was controlled by Italy. Algeria and Tunisia were ruled by the French, and Morocco was controlled by both the French and the Spanish. Today all are independent nations.

Algeria, Libya, Morocco, and Tunisia have much in common. They are all on the northern rim of the great African continent, bordering the Mediterranean Sea. But more important than their geographic similarity, is the fact that these nations share a common people, history, and way of life.

HISTORIC HOME OF
THE BARBARY PIRATES

Northern Africa was once called Barbary and these four nations were called the Barbary States. From this region the infamous Barbary pirates once sailed forth to attack and rob ships moving across the Mediterranean. As late as the nineteenth century the United States and other nations paid huge amounts of money to the Barbary States for protection from these pirates. Finally, when Thomas Jefferson was president, the United States Navy under Captain Stephen Decatur forced the Barbary rulers to stop these acts of piracy. Somewhat later the Barbary States were broken up and divided among France, Italy, and Spain.

Racially, the people of northern Africa were originally white or *Caucasian*, and the people of southern Africa were black or *Negroid*. Historically, about two-thirds of all Africans were black, and one-third was white. The two races were long separated by the world's largest desert, the Sahara, which runs across Africa from the Atlantic Ocean to the Red Sea. However, today many Africans are a mixture of both races.

For hundreds of years northern Africa was — and still is to a large degree — cut off from southern Africa by the vast, sandy wastes of the Sahara. North Africa had fairly easy access to Europe — it was not difficult to travel by boat on the warm, calm waters of the Mediterranean. Also, southern Europe was quite close. The Strait of Gibraltar, for example, which separates Spain from Morocco, is only about 15 miles (24 km) wide. Consequently, as will be clear in studying each of the former Barbary States separately, European influence has always been quite strong.

In learning about each of these nations in turn, we shall move from west to east, that is, from Morocco on the Atlantic through Algeria and Tunisia, and finally to Libya on the east.

MOROCCO

LOCATION AND CLIMATE

Morocco is located in a key strategic position at the western entrance to the Mediterranean Sea. Any nation controlling Morocco could easily block the narrow Strait of Gibraltar and thus prevent ships from entering or leaving the Mediterranean. Because of this, several European nations long tried to control this country. Today, however, Morocco is an independent constitutional monarchy. This means it is ruled by a king, but the nation has a written constitution and a legislature that is elected by the people.

Morocco has a landscape and climate more varied than that of much of the rest of Africa. Its coasts border both the Mediterranean and the Atlantic (in the north and northwest), and farming is widespread in the usually pleasant coastal climate.

Cutting through the country from southwest to northeast is the great wall of the rugged Atlas Mountains. Between these and another coastal range in the north called the Rif Mountains is a great fertile valley. Here people farm and raise livestock.

The slopes of the mountains receive enough rain to supply the lowlands with water during much of the year. But summers in the plains are apt to be hot and dry. On the northern slopes of the Atlas Mountains there are also great, dense forests. In the south, temperatures rise to as high as 130° F (54° C), but the air is dry and it is often quite cool in the evenings.

Morocco is bordered on the east by Algeria and on the south by the barren Sahara. In the southwest Morocco's border has to this day not yet been decided upon. Much of this area was originally controlled by Spain as a part of the province of Spanish Sahara or Spanish West Africa. Control of the area is still in dispute.

AREA, POPULATION, AND PRINCIPAL CITIES

Because its southwestern border is undecided, the exact area of Morocco cannot be stated. It is, however, about 166,000 square miles (429,940 sq km). It has a population of more than 16,000,000 people, two-thirds of whom live on farms and one-third of whom live in towns and cities. Most of the people are Arabs or Berbers, or a mixture of the two called Moors.

The nation's foreign population is estimated to be about 150,000, consisting mostly of French and Spanish.

Morocco's principal cities are the capital, Rabat, and the largest city, Casablanca, which has a population of somewhat more than 1,500,000. Both cities are located on the Atlantic Coast.

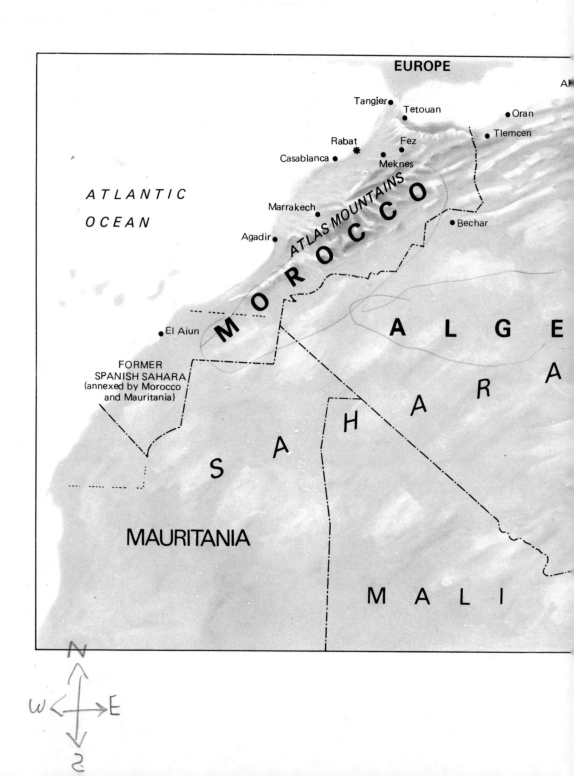

EUROPE

A

Tangier

Tetouan

Oran

Tlemcen

Rabat

Fez

Casablanca

Meknes

ATLANTIC
OCEAN

Marrakech

ATLAS MOUNTAINS

MOROCCO

Bechar

Agadir

El Aiun

ALGE

FORMER
SPANISH SAHARA
(annexed by Morocco
and Mauritania)

SAHARA

A

MAURITANIA

MALI

N

W E

S

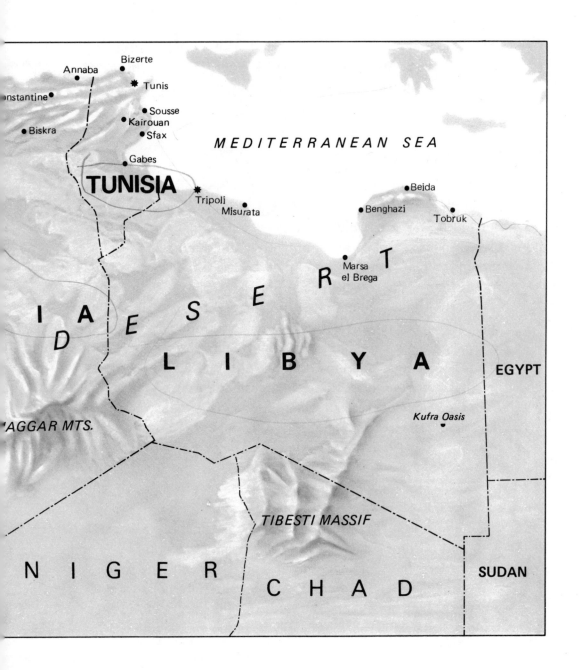

Other important cities (some of which the king uses as occasional capitals) include Marrakesh, Fez, and Tangier. Tangier, which was formerly an international zone, is the official summer capital.

TANGIER — CITY OF MYSTERY AND INTRIGUE

Tangier was long known as a city of espionage and intrigue. Part of this reputation was due to the imagination of its visitors. But much was justifiably based on the fact that the city once played an important part in international affairs, and soon became known as a place where government officials as well as espionage agents from many countries could mingle freely.

Early in this century, Great Britain, France, Italy, and Spain agreed to make Tangier and a few miles surrounding it into an International Zone in order to prevent its falling under the control of any one nation. For a time during World War II Spain occupied the city, but Spanish troops were forced to leave by the Allies. After the war an unsuccessful attempt was made to return Tangier to its international status, but the Soviet Union refused to allow this. Finally, in 1956, it was recognized as a part of the new kingdom of Morocco. The Tangier city governor is appointed by the Moroccan king. Today the city has a population of about 200,000, some 15,000 of whom are Moroccan Jews.

Tangier is just opposite Gibraltar and the Spanish coast at the west end of the Mediterranean. With its long, curving bay, it is one of Morocco's most important seaports, second only to Casablanca. Situated in a natural bowl-like valley, the white houses and the domes of its many mosques (Islamic places of worship) stand out against the surrounding hills. In the middle of the city is a place called the Casbah. In ancient times the Casbah was a walled fortress, but now it is mainly a marketplace and a section where many Arabs, Berbers, and Moors live.

LANGUAGES, RELIGION, AND EDUCATION

Morocco's main languages are Arabic, Berber, French, and Spanish. English is also widely spoken and understood. The nation's main religions are Islam and Roman Catholicism.

Although education is required for boys and girls between the ages of seven and thirteen, the inability to read and write remains high — about 85 percent — among the general population. In an attempt to combat this illiteracy, an effort has been made to teach the same subjects and give the same tests in all of Morocco's French, Spanish, Israeli, and Muslim schools. This effort at the standardization of the school system has met with considerable success in teaching the nation's more than one million students.

Arabic is taught in the primary schools for the first two years, and both Arabic and French are taught during the next three years. Lessons are also in both Arabic and French in the secondary schools.

Some 20,000 students attend Moroccan universities, the most important of which are at the capital city of Rabat and the historic city of Fez. The university at Fez was founded 1100 years ago.

HOW THE PEOPLE EARN A LIVING

Most Moroccans earn a living through a direct use of the nation's farm and forest land. About 70 percent of the population depend upon agriculture for their livelihood. Cereals — barley, wheat, and corn — are the most important crops grown, followed by grapes, citrus fruits, olives, almonds, and figs. Most crops are planted by hand, and they are cultivated by horse-drawn plows. Dates are grown in the south on desert oases, places in the desert where (because of underground water) trees and other plants can grow. Some of these oases are natural; others are created through irrigation.

In the mountainous parts of Morocco, the people live in villages in the mountain heights during the summer and farm and raise animals in the valleys below. Then in winter, just before the first snow arrives, the people all leave their villages with their sheep, goats, and cattle and move into the warmer valleys. In the spring they once again return to their mountain villages.

In the desert and semidesert areas of the south, there are many people called *nomads*. These people have no permanent homes but move about constantly, living in tents and making a living by raising camels and other animals. They sell these animals to the farmers in villages and on oases.

MINING, INDUSTRY, AND FISHING

Some Moroccans are also miners. The nation's mines produce phosphates, iron ore, lead, zinc, manganese, and hard coal. Limestone and marble are also quarried. Some petroleum (oil) is produced, but it is not as plentiful in Morocco as it is elsewhere in North Africa. Actually, in most years Morocco must import oil. Consequently, it is not a member of the Organization of Petroleum Exporting Countries (OPEC), an important economic organization in the Middle East.

An oasis in Morocco. Oases are desert areas made fertile by either natural underground springs or through irrigation projects.

Morocco imports much more of most things than it exports, but phosphates (used to make fertilizer) are a major export. In an average year Morocco exports several million metric tons of phosphates, ranking it third among the world's most important producers of this product. Only the United States and the Soviet Union produce more. All of the nation's phosphate mines are owned by the government as are the railways and electric utilities. As recently as 1963 there was much French-owned farm- and timberland as well as mining property, but this has since been taken over by the Moroccan government. Light industry, such as the manufacture of cement, leather goods and textiles, is growing steadily, and fisheries dot the coastal towns.

Local handicrafts include rug making, pottery making, fine metalwork, and leatherwork. Some of these products are exported, but most are sold to tourists. Moroccan handicrafts are displayed and sold in the city bazaars and are world famous. Tourism is big business in Morocco, with an average of over one million tourists visiting the nation each year.

HOW THE PEOPLE LIVE

Few Moroccan women work outside the home. In the cities more women now work for pay than did in the past, but most still spend all their time taking care of their home and children while their husband supplies the family's money. Under the nation's Constitution there is universal suffrage — that is, everyone has the right to vote — but few women do vote.

Living conditions in the cities are generally poor except for a privileged few people. Most cities are divided into sections called "quarters" where the various kinds of tradespeople live. These quarters date back to ancient times when the different trade groups or "guilds" occupied certain specified areas. Further divisions usually include a European area, a Jewish section, and an Arab-Berber, or Moorish, section called a *medina*.

The walls that still surround some cities also date back to ancient times. These walls were built for protection, and entry could be gained only through huge iron gates. Some of these ornate gates still exist as well.

Many poor workers live in run-down areas at the edge of the cities. Their homes are merely huts made of scraps of wood and sheet metal. The government has made great efforts to improve these conditions, but poverty still exists, especially in Casablanca.

Wealthy Moroccans as well as many foreigners live in handsome high-rise apartments and hotels, many of them along the coast. These brilliant, modern buildings give much of Morocco an attractive skyline that is one of the first things a tourist notices in approaching the country either by air or sea. Beyond this crust of prosperous beauty, however, are scenes of absolute poverty. In the affluent areas of the cities, streets are wide and pleasant. In the poor sections, the streets are more like alleys. A person standing in the middle of one of them can often stretch his or her arms and touch the shops and houses on either side. They are also crowded with men, women, children, and donkeys constantly surging through.

In the villages, as well as in some areas of the cities, people live in small houses made from sunbaked clay bricks. These are not unlike the adobe houses in Mexico and the southwestern United States. To keep out the dust and heat, many of these adobe

homes have no windows. And because of the dry climate, it is always dusty in Morocco. Houses in the mountain regions are built in tiers (levels) that follow the contours of the rising mountains. They almost seem to be built right on top of one another like apartment buildings.

Like the nomads, some farmers live in tents made from animal skins or woven animal hair and other fibers. Most, however, live in adobe houses or circular houses of wood with thatched straw roofs.

FOOD AND DRESS

Moroccans living in the cities or in villages or on farms have a fairly standard diet, usually including lamb, chicken, fish, citrus fruits, dates, nuts, and vegetables. They also drink goat's milk and eat a thick form of curdled milk called *yogurt*. Fresh, drinkable water is scarce everywhere and unobtainable in the Sahara region except at oases.

Modern Moroccans' dress is much like that of their ancestors although European and American fashions have had some influence on city dwellers. Traditional dress for men includes baggy trousers, long cotton shirts, a bright sash around the waist, and leather sandals. Their hat is called a fez, and is red, cone-shaped, and often made of felt.

This gateway to the city of Fez is part of the remains of an ancient protection wall that surrounded the city.

Women dress in much the same way. Their baggy trousers are topped by cotton or linen blouses which are also gathered at the waist by bright silk sashes. According to Islam custom, no one outside the home is supposed to see a woman's face. On the street most older Moroccan women wear full-length hooded cloaks that cover their entire body, head, and face except for their eyes. They too wear leather sandals. Today, however, some young Moroccan women wear more modern dress such as skirts or blue jeans and leave the veils to the older generation.

HISTORY AND GOVERNMENT

In ancient times the area that is now known as Morocco was a Roman province called Mauretania. When the Roman Empire fell, the area was ruled first by the Berbers and then by the Arabs, who came out of western Asia. Finally the Arabs and Berbers merged to form a powerful Moorish Empire. The Moors waged war against what is now Spain, Portugal, and France, and for several centuries control of the lands at the western end of the Mediterranean passed back and forth between the Moors on one side and the Spanish, Portuguese, and French on the other.

Moroccan pirates under a series of sultans (kings) were the main rulers between the fourteenth and nineteenth centuries. When their hold was broken, several European nations fought for control of the country. Finally, Morocco was divided into two areas that were protected by France and Spain from interference by other nations. These two so-called "protectorates" lasted from 1912 to 1956.

Moroccan independence grew out of World War II, which brought an end to most colonial empires. France and Spain reluctantly gave up their control of the country, and there was a considerable amount of rioting and bloodshed before independence was gained. Even when Moroccan independence was achieved, Spain held on to certain sections of the country at Ceuta, Melilla, and Ifni as well as the Western or Spanish Sahara. These areas within Morocco still ruled by Spain are called enclaves. It was not, in fact, until the late 1970s that a final transfer of power for a portion of Spanish Sahara was made from Spain to Morocco.

THE KINGDOM OF MOROCCO

When Morocco became independent, the country did not automatically become a democracy. It is, in fact, one of the last kingdoms in the world. It is a somewhat democratic kingdom, however, with a written constitution which was approved by the people in 1962 and modified in 1970.

Under the Moroccan Constitution there is a single chamber or *unicameral* legislature or parliament, which is at least partially chosen by general, free elections. But the king actually has absolute authority. He appoints the nation's prime minister, approves all legislation, and has the right at any time to dissolve parliament.

The reigning king in the late 1970s was Hassan II, who was born in 1929. His chosen successor is Crown Prince Sidi Muhammed, who was born in 1963.

Hassan is generally regarded by his own people as quite a democratic king. He has often said: "The purpose of good government is not to make the rich poor but to make the poor rich."

ALGERIA

For more than a century — from 1848 to 1962 — Algeria was French territory. Four times larger than France itself, Algeria is the largest of the four North African nations. It also had to fight harder than any of the other three for its independence.

Beginning shortly after World War II, there were bloody clashes between the Europeans in Algeria (mainly French at the time), and the Muslims for continued control of the country. These clashes developed into a vicious war that lasted for eight long years. More than one-half million Algerians were killed or wounded in the struggle. More than two million were made homeless. Many thousands of Muslims fled the country, most to seek refuge in Morocco and Tunisia.

Finally, French President Charles de Gaulle developed a plan to give Algeria its independence. This plan was adopted in 1962, and the country was turned over to the Algerians. But Algeria still suffers from this costly struggle, and physical, economic, and social signs of it are clearly visible in the nation today.

LOCATION AND CLIMATE

Algeria's location and its great riches in oil and natural gas have made it a prize worth fighting for. These oil and gas reserves — estimated at 10 percent of the world's total reserve supply — are located in the Sahara Desert to the south and east. Great pipelines carry the oil and gas to ports on the Mediterranean Sea in the north to be exported to other countries.

In addition to being bordered by the Mediterranean in the north and the Sahara in the south and east, Algeria touches seven other nations. These include Morocco, Spanish Sahara, Mauritania, and Mali to the west and southwest. On the east and southeast are Tunisia, Libya, and Niger.

The climate in a narrow strip along the Mediterranean is generally pleasant. Inland, however, temperatures soar to well over the 100° F (38° C) level both winter and summer.

The coastal strip is called the Tell, which in Arabic means "hill." It is about 50 miles (80.65 km) wide and 600 miles (967.74 km) long. Within this strip there are vast vineyards where grapes for wine are grown. Wine is one of the nation's major exports. There are also orchards of olive, fig, and citrus fruit trees. Some cereal grains, tobacco, and cotton are also grown in this area.

Off the coast there are important fisheries where sardines, anchovies, and shellfish are caught. Most of the fish is locally canned for both domestic use and export.

(19)

The Atlas Mountains extend from Morocco into Algeria south of the coastal strip. Within the mountains there is a vast lake-studded plateau. Wheat and barley are grown in this region as well as a grass called *esparto*, which is used in manufacturing paper. Cork oak trees and cedar trees are also abundant on the northern slopes of the mountains facing the sea. On the dry southern mountain slopes Arab and Berber shepherds raise sheep, cattle, goats, and camels.

South of the Atlas Mountains lies the huge and barren Sahara. It occupies two-thirds of Algeria. In this virtually water-less area date palms grow at oases and yield the only valuable crop from this desert area.

AREA, POPULATION, AND PRINCIPAL CITIES

Algeria's area is 919,352 square miles (2,381,124 sq. km). It has a population of slightly more than sixteen million, most of whom are Arabs and Berbers with the Berbers outnumbering the Arabs about three to one. Before the revolution that brought Algeria independence, there was a large European population, mainly French. After the revolution, however, most left Algeria and returned to France. But the French influence is still strong, especially in the architectural styles in Algeria's major cities.

Jews formerly made up a large part of the population, but with the establishment of the nation of Israel after World War II, many Jews fled to Israel during the Algerian revolution. Today there are about 150,000 Jews in Algeria, most of them in the large cities.

Two of Algeria's major cities lie along the Mediterranean

(20)

Almost two-thirds of the total area of Algeria is
part of the Sahara Desert. While camels are slowly
being replaced by jeeps and trucks, they are
still quite common in most Middle East deserts.

coast. They are the capital, Algiers, with a population of about one million, and Oran, with a population of about 400,000. Both are important seaports. Constantine, with a population of about 300,000, is an important inland city.

Algiers has one of the largest and most interesting casbahs in the Middle East. In Arabic the word *casbah* means "citadel," and the casbah in Algiers is built on the heights of the oldest part of the city. Here the markets, mosques, and Moorish-style buildings are the hub of the capital city's picturesque Muslim life.

LANGUAGE, RELIGION AND EDUCATION

Algeria's official language is Arabic, but French and English are widely spoken. The nation's main religion is Islam, but there are a number of Roman Catholics left from the French period. In addition to the diminishing number of Jews and Jewish rabbis, there is a small and scattered number of Protestants and Protestant pastors.

Illiteracy is high in Algeria, averaging about 80 percent in the coastal area and more than 90 percent among desert dwellers. Only slightly more than half of the children attend school. There are more than 7,000 primary and elementary schools and about 800 secondary schools, but few Muslims attend schools beyond the primary and lower elementary levels.

There is one large and important university at Algiers with an enrollment of 14,000 students. New universities have been opened at Oran, Constantine, and Annaba.

To combat illiteracy and raise the level of education, the

government has adopted a series of Four-Year Plans. During these scheduled four-year periods — the second one ended in 1977 — new schools are being built, additional teachers are being trained, and an attempt at compulsory education is being made. In addition, vocational and technical schools are being established to train local boys and girls for jobs in the oil and gas fields as well as in local business and industry.

HOW THE PEOPLE EARN A LIVING

Most of Algeria has limited use as far as farming is concerned. The most valuable farmland is in the Tell area where there are highly fertile plains and valleys. This area was formerly broken up into farms and ranches owned by the more than a million European colonists. The holdings of the French landlords amounted to some 7,000,000 acres (2,830,000 hectares) of vineyards, orchards, and wheat fields. This was a third of the nation's good farmland and netted the French owners some $250 million a year. This left the poorer agricultural areas to be farmed by a million illiterate Algerians who had to struggle merely to produce enough food to survive.

When the colonists returned to France after the revolution, their farms were taken over by the Algerian government and turned into "Socialist Production Units." These cooperative farms are today run by groups of workers called self-management committees under a director appointed by the central government. Farmers' produce is sold through government marketing organizations.

At first this form of self-management was unsuccessful be-

A marketplace at El-Harrach, Algeria

cause few of the workers had enough technical skill or knowledge to run large farming operations. As the workers have gained skill and knowledge, however, there has been marked improvement in crop production. But government-controlled agriculture is still operating at a loss, so workers earn little beyond survival wages, a part of which are paid in produce.

An equally serious agricultural problem is how to improve the production of individual farms in unfertile areas where most of the people live. On these desperately poor single-family farms, many Muslims continue to struggle for a bare existence. In the villages located in these poverty stricken rural areas, at least half of the work force is unemployed.

FOOD, DRESS, HOUSING, AND RECREATION

In general, the daily life of the Algerians, both in the countryside and in the cities, is similar to that of the Moroccans. They eat similar food, wear much the same clothing, and live in the same kinds of homes. There are, however, more veiled girls and women than in any other North African country. This probably represents a strong desire to return to the old ancestral ways encouraged by a reaction against French modernization. Exceptions are found among the university students who generally follow European ways and customs in their dress and general life-style.

LIFE IN THE CITY

For several years after Algeria gained its independence, most city dwellers were no better off than the people living in remote rural areas. But in recent years great efforts have been made by the government to increase industrial development, and these efforts have just begun to be successful. Algerian mines produce phosphates, iron, lead, and zinc, and tremendous strides forward have been made in the manufacture of steel. There is a huge iron and steel complex at Annaba, and production there will soon take care of all domestic needs. Other large steelworks are being built in western Algeria.

Additional major industrial projects include a huge petro-chemical complex, the further development of the country's iron mines, an ammonia plant, truck and farm machinery manufactur-ing plants, and shipbuilding. All of these projects have helped provide badly needed jobs for the unemployed working popu-lation in urban areas.

Financing this industrial effort has been a major problem, and it has been done largely at the expense of the rural popu-lation on whom little government money has been spent. France originally agreed to provide the necessary funds for industrial development but never entirely fulfilled the agreement. One result of this involved many thousands of poor people who moved into the cities from rural areas in the hopes they would find bet-ter jobs. When there were no jobs immediately available, the newcomers were simply added to the huge numbers of those already unemployed.

Since the new Algerian government was pledged to take care of the needs of all of the people, many unemployed were allowed to live rent-free in the homes and apartment buildings formerly occupied by the French. This situation has been recently much improved, mainly through the growth in industry. This

The capital of Algeria, Algiers, is situated
on the shores of the Mediterranean Sea.

growth has been tremendous, not only in iron and steel but also in the production of oil and natural gas.

BLACK GOLD FROM THE DESERT

Oil was discovered in the Sahara Desert area of Algeria only a quarter of a century ago. In the late 1950s several large oil fields went into production, and shortly after this "black gold" began to flow from the desert, natural gas was also discovered there. Pipelines to carry these potential riches to ports at Oran and Algiers were completed a short time later. Within these few years annual oil production has reached an average of almost a million barrels a day. Annual natural gas production averages more than 13,500,000 cubic meters. By the 1980s Algeria is expected to be the world's largest producer of natural gas. Like oil, natural gas can be shipped in tankers in liquid form. This is done by chilling gas until it liquefies. Reheated, it becomes a gas. Liquefied natural gas is usually referred to as LNG.

Among the thirteen member nations of the Organization of Petroleum Exporting Countries, Algeria is the tenth-ranking producer. It does not, however, receive all of the money that is paid for its oil and LNG. According to an agreement with France, Algeria receives just half of the revenue from the wells. The French government receives the rest because it loaned Algeria the money to develop the oil fields and pipelines. Several American and British oil companies also retained rights to some of the wells along with permission to explore for new ones. But their share of the profits is much less than Algeria's and is steadily being reduced.

LIFE IN THE OIL FIELDS

Gradually, the oil fields are being "Algerianized." This means more and more Algerian workers and technicians are taking over jobs formerly held by foreigners. And salaries in the oil camps are ideal — although working conditions for the drilling crews and manual workers are extremely difficult. Manual workers earn more in one month than the three-quarters of a million desert dwellers earn in one year.

The oil camps are isolated and self-contained. They are like small, air-conditioned oases in the heart of the burning Sahara desert, a vast area that is more than twice as big as Texas. Here, in the heart of the otherwise unlivable desert, air-conditioned trailers house the oil crews and their supervisors. Often they have their families with them. There are nightly movies, and good food and wine are flown in from as far away as France. There are also swimming pools and tennis courts housed in air-conditioned buildings.

The crews spend four weeks on the job and then have one week off. For their week off they are flown to coastal cities or even to France. Many crews like to spend their week's leave in Paris. Then it is back to the desert and the never-ending task of working to get oil for an energy-hungry world.

Workers on the oil rigs put in eight- to ten-hour shifts around the clock since pumping oil or drilling for it goes on twenty-four hours a day. Other oil company employees work from six to eleven in the morning and from three to six in the afternoon, thus avoiding the worst heat in the middle of the day. Outside the air-conditioned sanctuary of the trailers and buildings, the blazing heat threatens to dehydrate the workers. To prevent this they drink as much as five gallons of water a day.

FORMER HOME OF THE FRENCH FOREIGN LEGION

The Algerian Sahara is also the former home of the famed French Foreign Legion. There are still, in fact, a few outposts in the Sahara today. Founded in France in 1831 by King Louis Philippe, the Legion had its headquarters at Sidi-bel-Abbès, Algeria. The corps was made up of foreign volunteers for service outside France, and its original purpose was the conquest of Algeria.

Because recruiting officers for the Legion asked no questions about the background of recruits wanting to join its ranks, the Legion became a home for criminals and political exiles as well as just plain adventurers. After serving in the Legion for five years, a Legionnaire could become a French citizen. Pay was low, discipline was strict, and living conditions were hard. Nevertheless, there was fighting and adventure aplenty, and the Legion never lacked volunteers.

When Algeria gained its independence in 1962, Legion headquarters were moved to Aubagne, France. Some units were left behind in the Sahara to maintain peace and order among the various tribespeople and to protect the oil and gas fields. Today the Legion is just another unit in the French army and the traditional uniform of baggy red trousers and high-collar blue coat has been exchanged for a far less vivid uniform of brown khaki. But the Legion's legendary memory lingers on in the Sahara.

HISTORY

Like Morocco, Algeria was originally a Roman province. Roman rule lasted for about four hundred years. What is now Algeria then fell to the Vandals from Europe who were in turn driven out by the Arabian Muslims. The Moors then established Algeria as one of the Barbary States.

In its warfare against the Barbary pirates, France seized Oran and built a fortress near Algiers. The Algerians then turned to the Turks for help. Turkey soon ejected the French and took over the country, installing a governor at Algiers. But France did not give up its efforts to regain control.

THE WAR CAUSED BY A FLYSWATTER

Following the wars against the Barbary pirates, France reopened trade negotiations with the Turks at Algiers in 1827. During the course of these negotiations, the Turkish governor struck the French consul with a flyswatter. This incident inflamed the French public, and France sent a naval expedition to drive the Turks out of Algiers. The French also seized several other coastal cities but were less successful in gaining control of inland Algeria.

Finally, with the help of the newly formed French Foreign Legion, France conquered the whole of Algeria by 1848. It was many years, however, before military rule was replaced by civil administration. Toward the end of the nineteenth century Algeria was allowed to send representatives to the French Parliament in Paris where they could take part in decisions about colonial rule. But self-government was still a long way off.

During World War II Algeria was thrust into the conflict when the Allies invaded Oran and other points along the coast. Algeria became the base for Charles de Gaulle's Free French Government as well as the base for the Allies in their campaign to drive the Germans and Italians out of North Africa.

After the war all Algerian Muslims won the right to become French citizens, and all adults, including Muslim women, gained the right to vote. But the winds of change were blowing through North Africa, and the spirit of independence was in the air.

THE REVOLUTION

When France refused to give Algeria its independence, the Algerians formed a revolutionary party in 1951. It was called the National Liberation Front (FLN). In 1954 the FLN went to war against both the French civil administration and the French army. In 1958 a free Algerian government was formed at Cairo, Egypt. This government was to take over control of Algeria as soon as the French were driven out.

In 1961 French President de Gaulle called for a referendum in France and Algeria to decide whether or not Algeria should be given its independence. The people voted to give Algeria its freedom, and President de Gaulle declared that Algeria was independent on July 3, 1962.

GOVERNMENT

Unfortunately, unrest continued in Algeria for several years. In 1963 Ahmed Ben Bella was declared president of the new Democratic People's Republic of Algeria. But he and his government were soon overthrown by a group of army officers who formed a so-called Revolutionary Council to run the country. In 1965 Colonel Houari Boumedienne was chosen to head this council. In 1976 Boumedienne was given a further six-year term as president.

Boumedienne brought a degree of democracy to his socialistic government by allowing general elections to the National People's Assembly (a form of parliament) in late 1977. Almost 80 percent of the electorate voted to elect 261 members to the assembly. The growth of political freedom in Algeria doubtless depends on the country's continued economic growth and the stability of Boumedienne's regime.

TUNISIA

In many ways Tunisia is a much more modern and progressive nation than either Morocco or Algeria. While Moroccans and Algerians are somewhat inclined to look to the past and cling to ancestral ways and customs, Tunisians tend to welcome that which is modern and new. Consequently, Tunisia is something of a North African showplace of economic and social development.

This forward-looking philosophy undoubtedly stems from the fact that, historically, Tunisia was the crossroads of the ancient world. And it is still very much of a crossroads and hub of commerce and political activity in the Middle East today.

Occupying a long, narrow strip of land in northern Africa, Tunisia is roughly divided into three geographical regions.

LOCATION AND CLIMATE

The Atlas Mountains extend from Morocco and Algeria into Tunisia and make up the country's northern region. This region has fertile valleys and plains that extend down to the Mediterranean. Cork oak, pine, and cedar trees are grown on the mountain slopes where rain is plentiful.

In the northern valleys and plains grapes and cereal crops — corn, wheat, and barley — are cultivated. In addition, there are sizable plantations on the Cap Bon peninsula where oranges, lemons, and tangerines are grown. Olive trees are also abundant in a part of this region called the *Sahel*. The climate is semitropical and considerably cooler than it is inland.

The central region is occupied by high tablelands which are excellent for grazing sheep, goats, cattle, and camels. Figs and orchard fruits such as apricots, peaches, and apples are also grown in this region. The climate here is dry and hot, ranging from 85°–100° F (30°–40° C) in the summer to 50°–70° F (10°–20° C) in the winter.

The southern region is occupied principally by the Sahara Desert where dates are grown at oases. This is also where most of Tunisia's oil wells and some of its natural gas wells are located. Temperatures soar to as high as 140° F (60° C) in the Tunisian Sahara.

AREA, POPULATION, AND
PRINCIPAL CITIES

Tunisia covers an area of about 63,362 square miles (164,108 sq. km), and has a population of slightly more than 5,500,000. Its

A class in introductory economics at a school outside
the city of Tunis. Great progress has been made in recent
years in the struggle to eliminate illiteracy in Tunisia.

capital and largest city is Tunis, with a population of about 1,000,000. Carthage, one of the greatest cities of the ancient world and a rival of imperial Rome, is now a suburb of Tunis.

Sfax (pop. 475,000) and Sousse (pop. 225,000) are walled cities and important seaports. Bizerte (pop. 62,000) is another seaport on the Mediterranean with an excellent natural port. It was formerly one of France's largest and most important naval and military bases in North Africa.

Kairouan (pop. 54,000) is a holy city of the Muslims that is of sacred importance throughout the Islamic world. Kairouan is surrounded by walls more than 1,000 years old and is the site of one of Islam's most famous mosques. Mecca in Saudi Arabia is the chief holy city of the Muslims. It is where Mohammed, founder of the Islamic religion, was born. Mohammed taught his followers that one of their five duties was to make a pilgrimage or *hajj* to Mecca. If Muslims cannot afford a trip to Mecca or cannot go there for some other reason, a pilgrimage to Kairouan's central mosque is regarded as a suitable substitute.

LANGUAGES, RELIGION, AND EDUCATION

The official language is Arabic, but French and English are widely spoken.

Islam is the official religion, but there are also a number of Roman Catholics, most of whom are French.

Literacy is relatively high in Tunisia — about 40 percent — as compared with the other North African nations. The state controls all of the schools through its Ministry of National Education, and great efforts have been made to stamp out illiteracy. These efforts have been successful except in remote rural areas and among the nomadic tribes of the desert where illiteracy still approaches 90 percent.

The proportion of the Tunisian government's budget devoted to education is very high — about 25 percent, while only 6 percent goes to the military. In Algeria, by comparison, these budget figures are almost exactly reversed. While universal education is not yet compulsory, all education is free from the primary grades on through the university level. About 60 percent of young people between the ages of five through nineteen attend school. This is double the number of young people who were in school when the French ruled the country.

HOW THE PEOPLE EARN A LIVING

Tunisia's chief industry is agriculture, with half the population living in rural farming areas. (About 60 percent of the country is suitable for farming.) Much of the agricultural work is done on large cooperative farms, owned and managed by the state, with workers' committees having only limited authority in their day-to-day operation. Lack of knowledge about how to run large farming operations long hampered productivity, but recently agricultural production has been on the rise. This is a direct result of increased training and education received by farmers in modern agriculture methods as well as the wide use of phosphates for fertilizer.

Most privately owned farms in Tunisia are small, and their output is seldom more than enough to support their owners. This

A young farm worker at Kairouan

(38)

difference in income between the small farmer and those on the large plantations has created a serious economic problem for the nation.

An inadequate water supply is another of Tunisia's serious agricultural problems. This will be largely solved for northern Tunisia with the completion of a huge dam at Joumine, which is being financed by the Soviet Union. Within the next several years this dam will furnish water for irrigation through a series of canals. The mining and exporting of phosphates, iron, lead, zinc and potash also add to the country's income.

OIL AND NATURAL GAS

The Tunisian economy is highly dependent on its oil and natural gas. Oil was first discovered in the Tunisian Sahara in 1964, and natural gas was discovered several years later in the Sahara and off the coast near Gabes. Offshore oil was discovered at about this time. Oil production has since reached well over 150,000 barrels a day, and reserves have been estimated at 185,000,000 barrels. Natural gas reserves are estimated at 150,000,000,000 cubic meters.

To date not all of the offshore natural gas has been used because it has been uneconomical to bring it ashore. But the construction of underseas pipelines will soon alter this situation. One such pipeline is now under construction from Algeria to Italy via Tunisia's Cap Bon and the island of Sicily.

More than three-quarters of Tunisia's oil is exported. Most of it is sold to Italy, the money from which helped finance Tunisia's main refinery at Bizerte. That refinery is now being expanded, and a new refinery is to be built at Gabes in 1978.

While Tunisia does export some oil, the amount is not large enough to make it a member of the Organization of Petroleum Exporting Countries. Nevertheless, it is sufficiently large to support the rest of the nation's industrial economy. This includes the expansion of its manufacturing industry. Major new manufacturing plants include a sugar refinery, steel plants, a marble finishing plant, textile and leather factories, and an automobile and truck tire factory.

Tourism also adds a substantial sum to the nation's economy, and the government has done much to promote it. More than a million people a year, not including ships' passengers who merely visit the port cities, come to Tunisia as tourists. The country has one of the best road and railway networks in the Middle East, which greatly aids travel. Its hotels are also outstanding, and its people are eager to make friends with foreigners.

HOW THE PEOPLE LIVE

The standard of living is high in Tunisia when compared with that of the other countries of North Africa. People in rural areas live much as the people live in the rural areas of Morocco and Algeria. They also wear similar clothes, eat the same kind of food, and engage in similar forms of recreation.

The people in the cities, however, tend to adapt more to Western and European ways in their life-style. The Muslim religion and customs are not so dutifully followed here as elsewhere in the Muslim world. In fact, the government has actively encouraged a modernization of the Muslim religion. One of its reasons for doing so has been a desire to do away with the fatalistic Muslim idea that no matter how hard men or women try, they cannot

A residential section of Tunis, the capital of Tunisia.

better their lot in life. The modern Tunisian government has tried — and with considerable success — to instill in its citizens the idea that people can accomplish almost anything they want to do if they work hard enough. Motion pictures and television are extremely popular in Tunisian cities, and many people try to imitate the dress, customs, and way of life as shown in American and European movies.

One of Tunisia's major problems, however, is unemployment, especially in urban areas. All workers are guaranteed jobs of some kind, but government-sponsored jobs may be merely digging ditches and repairing roads on various public works projects. Although there are few signs of grinding poverty in the cities, there is a serious lack of good jobs. This has been brought about by the fact that people have flocked into the cities from the countryside faster than Tunisian industry has expanded.

The Tunisian government's most pressing problem is thus twofold: to make farming attractive and profitable enough to prevent too many rural people leaving their farms for the city; and to expand industry rapidly enough to take care of all those city dwellers seeking stimulating jobs.

Nevertheless, despite its problem areas, Tunisia's economic development in the less than a quarter of a century since it became independent has been one of the most successful in the Middle East.

HISTORY

The ancient city of Carthage on the site of modern Tunis was founded by the Phoenicians in the ninth century B.C. Rivalry between Carthage and Rome led to the destruction of Carthage in 146 B.C. After several centuries the Romans were driven out of Tunisia by the Vandals and in about the sixth century after Christ it became a part of the Byzantine Empire. In the seventh century a rebuilt Carthage was captured by the Arabs and again destroyed. It is these ruins that form a part of modern Tunis.

In the sixteenth century Turkey gained control of Tunisia, installing a governor there but giving the Tunisians a limited amount of self-government. It was under Turkish rule that Tunisia became a pirate stronghold along with the other Barbary States. In breaking the hold of the pirates on this area, France and Italy became rivals for control of Tunisia. France wanted to extend its Algerian borders to include Tunisia. Italy's claim on the country was based on the fact that a large number of Italians already lived there. Finally, French troops took over Tunisia in 1881, and the country became a French protectorate in 1883. French rule was to last until 1956.

During both World War I and World War II, Tunisia played a key role as a French naval base. For a time after the fall of France in World War II, the country was occupied by the Germans, but the Tunisians remained loyal to the French. However, after the war Tunisia began to demand its independence. Finally, in 1955, Tunisians gained partial self-government, and in 1956 France agreed to its complete independence.

GOVERNMENT

In the same year that it gained its independence, Tunisia elected its first legislature and adopted a constitution. The following year the legislature dethroned Tunisia's traditional monarch, and the nation became a republic. Its first president was Habib Bourguiba, who is still in office today.

Bourguiba has been a remarkably forward-looking leader, although he is referred to by many as a "benevolent despot." Immediately upon coming to power he made widespread civil reforms, including the acceptance of women's right to vote (for the first time in Tunisian history). He usually spends several months each year visiting and inspecting all parts of the country. In many towns and villages he knows some families by their names. These visits have led directly to slum clearance and the construction of new schools and public buildings. As late as 1974, Bourguiba announced that his nation would merge with Libya for the economic welfare of the people of both countries, but this plan has since been dropped.

TROUBLES WITH FRANCE AND EGYPT

In 1958 Tunisia became a member of the Arab League, an organization of Middle East countries designed to encourage and protect Arab interests. In spite of this, however, President Bourguiba has often differed with other Arab League members on certain issues. In 1967 Tunisia was not actively involved in the war between Israel and several Arab states. After the conflict ended, Bourguiba blamed Egypt for losing the war and accused it of trying to dominate all Arab affairs. In June of 1973 Bourguiba urged Arab peace negotiations with Israel, and he renewed his pleas for Arab-Israeli peace in 1978.

BOURGUIBA ELECTED FOR LIFE

Officially Tunisia is a sovereign independent republic. Actually, it is very much a socialist state with a dictator-like premier. There is only one legal political party, the Destourian Socialist Party. This party controls the press and conducts propaganda campaigns to promote public participation in all government programs. To date, however, the Destourian Socialist Party has not used brutal police state methods to stay in power.

President Bourguiba was reelected to office for a term of five to ten years in 1964. He was again reelected, this time for life, in 1974. The fact that Bourguiba and his nation's one political party have indeed been benevolent toward Tunisia has, to date, worked out well for all Tunisians. But what will happen to the benevolent dictatorship when Bourguiba dies — he was born in 1903 — is anyone's guess.

LIBYA

Libya is the only one of the four nations of North Africa that was controlled by the Italians rather than the French before World War II. Although Libya gained its independence about the same time as Morocco, Algeria, and Tunisia, it is the least democratic of the four nations. Nevertheless, the discovery of an enormously rich oil field in the Libyan desert area of the Sahara in the late 1950s caused an "oil revolution" that has resulted in economic growth and changes in Libya that have been among the most spectacular in North Africa.

LOCATION AND CLIMATE

More than 90 percent of Libya is made up of desert or semi-desert. This means that only the coastal area has a relatively pleasant Mediterranean climate, and elsewhere temperatures are typical of those found throughout the Sahara Desert regions of Morocco, Algeria, and Tunisia. Libya had a temperature of 136° F (58° C) officially recorded at Aziza on September 13, 1922. This was long held to be the highest temperature ever recorded, but even higher temperatures have since been unofficially reported in Tunisia and elsewhere in the Sahara.

Libya's northern border is formed by the Mediterranean Sea. This coastline extends for about 1,000 miles (1,613 km.) To the west Libya is bordered by Tunisia and Algeria, and to the east, Egypt and Sudan. On the south lie Niger and Chad.

AREA, POPULATION, AND PRINCIPAL CITIES

Libya has an area of 679,358 square miles (1,759,539 sq km), and a population of about 2,500,000, most of whom are Arabs and Berbers. There are, however, many Europeans, especially Italians.

The most important cities are Tripoli, the capital, with a population of about half a million; Benghazi (pop. 282,000), and Misurata (pop. 103,000). All cities are important ports.

LANGUAGES, RELIGION, AND EDUCATION

As in most Arab countries, Arabic is the official language and Islam the official religion although other religions are allowed. Muslim customs are rigidly followed. For example, the use of alcohol is forbidden, and it is illegal to bring it into the country.

Early education is compulsory, and there is a universal system of education through the primary and elementary grades.

Nevertheless, illiteracy for the country as a whole is high, averaging over 80 percent.

About 10,000 people attend the Libyan University at Benghazi with a branch at Tripoli. They study the fine arts, teaching methods, economics, and engineering. Many young Libyans study abroad at foreign universities. Also in Tripoli there are schools for foreign students whose parents work for American, British, French, Dutch, and Italian oil companies operating in Libya.

HOW THE PEOPLE EARN A LIVING

Before the discovery of oil, agriculture was Libya's most important industry. About 80 percent of the people are still engaged in farming, but they are limited to the narrow fringe of land along the Mediterranean and to numerous oases. The oases near the Mediterranean are the richest in North Africa. Here dates, olives, and oranges are grown as well as almonds, apricots, and figs.

The western region of the coastal fringe is called Tripolitania. Here cereal crops — mainly barley, which makes up much of the Arab diet, and wheat — are grown along with cotton, tobacco, and some citrus fruits. The eastern region of the coastal fringe is called Cyrenaica. It has little or no fertile coastal plain but nevertheless dates and olives and some barley are grown by dry farming methods and irrigation.

"IF ONLY WE HAD FOUND WATER"

As in most Middle East countries, lack of water is a problem throughout Libya. Average annual rainfall at Tripoli, for example, is only 13 inches (33 cm), and there are years of severe drought

along the coast when even less rain falls. Although the discovery of oil has brought great riches to many Libyans, most farmers say, "If only we had found water instead of oil." In addition to dry farming, oases have been created by sinking deep wells below the water table which underlies most of Libya.

Just behind the fertile coastal area lies a dry plateau that provides excellent pastureland for grazing sheep, goats, donkeys, cattle, and camels. Like the North African Arabs in Morocco, Algeria, and Tunisia, the Libyans find the camel useful not only for transportation, but they also eat its meat and drink its milk.

LIFE IN THE COUNTRY AND CITY

The life of the average Libyan farmer is harsh. In their small, rude huts or tents, people and animals often live together. Donkeys can occasionally be seen peering out the glassless windows of adobe huts. Sheep, goats, and chickens run about the barren, sandy yard in front of the dwelling place, and they occasionally wander inside.

Many rural people who have come to the cities to seek jobs in the booming construction industry have somewhat improved their lot, but living conditions there can also be severe. Thousands live in shantytowns called *barrakas* where there are no electric lights, no flush toilets, and no running water for drinking or washing. Some live in mud huts with grass roofs. Others live in crude houses made of sheet metal, wood, and tarpaper.

The palm-lined waterfront promenade
in Tripoli along the Mediterranean Sea

Although Libyan women gained the right to vote in 1963, they still lead highly restricted lives. Most still wear veils. Many seldom leave their homes unless their husbands accompany them, and men and women rarely mix socially outside the family circle. Child brides and marriages arranged by families of the bride and groom are not uncommon even today.

The spectacular growth of the oil industry, however, is creting changes in these customs just as it is gradually improving the standard of living and creating other changes throughout the whole of Libyan society. Young women working as clerks, typists, secretaries, and receptionists for the oil companies have discarded their veils, and many have adopted Western dress, including skirts and slacks.

THE BOOMING OIL INDUSTRY

Oil was discovered in the Libyan Desert in 1959, and within two years it was being produced and exported. By 1968 Libya was producing almost 7 percent of the world's oil and supplying more than a third of Western Europe's needs. Its peak production was in 1970 when more than 3,000,000 barrels a day were produced, earning Libya some $1,300,000,000 for the year. Since then production has slacked off somewhat because of a lower worldwide demand for oil brought about by poor economic conditions. But Libya's earnings have skyrocketed due to the increased sales price of oil demanded by the OPEC nations. In 1974 Libya's earnings from oil were seven times greater than they were in 1970, and they have remained so through the late 1970s. Libya's oil is of very high quality, which is one of the reasons why it has been able to command a high price in the marketplace.

Although it is not as big an oil producer as most of the other OPEC nations, Libya has nonetheless been a leader in uniting the members of OPEC in their stand against the Western nations' continued control of Middle East oil. Libya was among the first of the Arab oil states to nationalize its oil industry, taking over ownership of companies that had formerly been in the hands of the Dutch, British, French, Italians, and Americans. It also led the way in raising prices on oil following the Arab oil embargo in 1973. In addition, Libya has been a leader in attempts to get the OPEC nations to conserve oil because its leaders are well aware that one day the oil will run out.

Today Libya has its own oil company, the Libyan National Oil Corporation (LINOCO). It explores and drills for oil, transports it via pipelines, and processes it at refineries for export aboard tankers. Any foreign nations wanting to engage in the oil business in Libya must work out an agreement with LINOCO — usually on terms that give Libya 85 percent of all profits.

HOW THE OIL MONEY IS USED

To date, oil revenues have largely been used to increase Libya's military strength. However, large amounts have also been spent on the improvement of agriculture and the building of new factories, oil refineries, ports, a merchant fleet, schools, hospitals, and other public works. In its most recent national development plan, which is to end in 1980, the government is planning on spending millions of dollars for the further improvement of agriculture, industry, roads, and housing.

One of Libya's major problems in the industrial area is the fact that much of its work force is made up of foreign workers. Because Libyan workers are largely untrained and unskilled, as much as 40 percent of the nation's industrial work force must be imported from Egypt and southern Europe. The Libyan government is struggling to overcome this handicap with free vocational and technical training offered to all who desire it.

The government has also been faced with the problem of Libyans spending their money on luxury consumer goods manufactured in other countries. Even many of the raw materials to be used in building new plants and homes must be purchased abroad. This causes a seriously unbalanced economy, but so far the government has not come up with any wholly satisfactory solution.

HISTORY

In ancient times the area that is now Libya was colonized by both the Phoenicians and the Greeks. In fact, the Greeks called the whole of North Africa — excluding Egypt — Libya. They thought that all of the people who lived in North Africa looked alike, and they gave them the name *Lebu*. Actually, the Lebu people were those who are today known as Berbers. The country was divided into two major provinces, Tripolitania and Cyrenaica. The Phoenicians occupied Tripolitania, and the Greeks occupied Cyrenaica.

All of Libya was then ruled in turn by the Egyptians, Romans, Vandals, Arabs, and Turks. Along the coast the Romans built one of their most beautiful colonial cities, called Leptis Magna. Nearby were two other Roman towns called Sabratha and Oea. The area was thus called Tripoli or "Three Cities." It was under the Turks that Tripoli became the headquarters of the Barbary pirates.

Early in the twentieth century, in 1912, Italy took possession of Libya after winning a war against the Turks. Tripolitania and Cyrenaica became official provinces within the Italian kingdom, and the southern desert region called the Fezzan was made into an Italian military district.

Italy did a great deal to improve conditions in Libya, mainly because it wanted to settle many thousands of Italian families there. Irrigation projects were begun, new roads were built, ports were improved, and farm machinery was sent there. Nevertheless, the Libyans deeply resented the Italian occupation and colonization and formed a resistance movement to gain their independence.

During World War I the Libyans, aided by the Turks, almost drove the Italians out of the country. But when Turkey was forced to withdraw from Africa after the Central Powers were defeated, Libya was left to carry on its fight for independence on its own.

LIBERATION IN WORLD WAR II

Libya was liberated from Italian rule in World War II. It had been one of the main battlegrounds for control of North Africa in that war. Early in the war the British fought both Italian and German troops in numerous fierce desert battles across the rim of North Africa. Key Libyan cities changed hands many times. Finally the Italians and Germans were driven out of Libya with thousands of Italian troops surrendering. Libya was then temporarily placed under British and French rule.

After the war the victorious Allied Powers could not agree on Libya's future. Italy was forced to give up control of the country, but its destiny could not otherwise be agreed upon. Finally it was left up to the United Nations to decide. In 1949 and 1950 the

United Nations decided that Libya should become an independent constitutional monarchy, and in 1951 Libya officially become an independent nation.

The first ruler of the new United Kingdom of Libya was Mohammed Idris Al-Senussi, who had been a leader of the Libyan resistance movement. King Idris reigned until 1969 when he was dethroned and forced into exile in Egypt by a group of Libyan army officers.

GOVERNMENT

Today Libya is ruled by several of the army officers who deposed King Idris and formed a ruling body called the Revolutionary Command Council. The council is assisted by a civilian cabinet. The actual head of state is Colonel Mu'ammar al-Gaddafi, chairman of the Revolutionary Command Council. The only legal political party is the Arab Socialist Union.

Between the early 1950s and late 1960s, under King Idris, Libya was divided into three provinces: Tripolitania, Cyrenaica, and Fezzan. Each was ruled by a governor appointed by the king, and assisted by a council elected by the people. However, the military rulers abolished this somewhat democratic system of govern-

These tribal leaders from a town in Libya relax with a traditional game after meeting to discuss community problems involving education, housing, and hygiene.

ment in 1963. Today the country is divided into ten separate districts each of which is administered by a commissioner. Each of these commissioners is directly responsible to the Revolutionary Command Council and the nation's actual military dictator, Colonel Gaddafi.

Libya's military leaders claim peaceful intentions toward all of the other nations of the Middle East. But late in 1977 and early in 1978 the government of the country of Chad accused Libya of attempting to take over its uranium-rich northern region that borders Libya.

The plans of the early 1970s to merge Libya and Tunisia have been dropped. More recently, however, plans have been made to merge Libya and Egypt. These plans to create a single, unified state were still being considered in the late 1970s. Their fulfillment depends somewhat on the outcome of the continuing Arab-Israeli conflict.

THE FUTURE FOR
NORTH AFRICA

The growth and development of the four nations of North Africa during the 1980s clearly depend upon several things: (1) a peaceful solution to the Arab-Israeli conflict; (2) improved world economic conditions; (3) workable worldwide energy conservation programs, especially on the part of the industrial nations of the West, so that oil reserves will last as long as possible. These problems are all closely related.

In recent years there has been almost constant conflict or the threat of conflict between several of the Arab nations and Israel. Twice, in 1967 and 1973, actual wars have broken out, and the threat of new wars remains. Many people have wondered if the Arab world really wants peace with Israel.

In 1977 and 1978 President Anwar el-Sadat of Egypt indicated that at least part of the Arab world not only was ready to accept Israel's existence as a nation, but also wanted it to exist in peace. Sadat's personal peace mission to Israel and the peace talks that followed were rays of hope in a dark Middle East situation. But when Israeli Prime Minister Menachem Begin refused to agree on certain territorial demands, the dark clouds of war once again seemed to hover over the Middle East.

There is little doubt that the Arabs have used oil as a political as well as an economic weapon in the Arab-Israeli conflict. The Arab threat to declare an oil embargo again is enough to give the Western industrial nations second thoughts about openly taking sides in the dispute. But the Arabs cannot always agree among themselves which side they are truly on. Egypt wants a peaceful settlement. Jordan, Syria, and Lebanon are flatly opposed to peaceful moves. In North Africa, Morocco and Tunisia would probably prefer peace at whatever cost. Algeria stands somewhere in between, supporting first one side and then the other. And Libya, despite its long-term efforts at close friendship with Egypt, opposed Sadat's friendly gestures toward Israel.

Of this much, North Africa as well as the rest of Africa can be sure: an all-out and lengthy Arab-Israeli war might very well mean total disaster. Such a conflict might bring both the Soviet Union and United States into the war on opposing sides. Both have major economic stakes in the area — not the least of which is oil — and a dreaded nuclear holocaust could result.

WHAT HAPPENS WHEN
THE OIL RUNS OUT?

When the Arab oil states temporarily cut off shipments of oil to countries supporting Israel in 1973, the industrial nations began to wonder what they would do when all of the world oil reserves were used up and there was no more oil to be had. After the embargo was lifted, this question still existed, but circumstances did not make it one of such immediate concern.

Soon the world seemed once again awash with oil, and the OPEC nations began to build up reserves of oil already produced and cut back on their petroleum production. But all energy experts have agreed that this is just a temporary situation. Eventually the oil will run out. No one, however, agrees when this will be. Estimates range from the late 1990s to the mid 2000s and even well beyond.

The problem of eventual OPEC oil depletion is, of course, as serious to the nations that export oil as it is to nations that must import some or all of their oil. This is especially true of several of the North African nations — Algeria, Tunisia, and Libya. These nations were extremely poor before oil was discovered within their borders. In the relatively brief time since then, they have begun to improve their economic condition and standard of living with money from oil revenues.

Even Morocco has received indirect benefits from the sudden prosperity of nearby states due to increased spending by visiting Algerians, Tunisians, and Libyans. Sales of Moroccan phosphate fertilizers have also greatly increased as the rest of North Africa has spent its oil money to improve agriculture.

In the immediate sense it is therefore important to North Africa that world economic conditions improve so that oil can continue to be sold at high prices. This will mean that economic conditions inside each of the North African countries can also continue to improve.

In the long run, however, it is essential that North African oil reserves not be used up before each of the four nations has a chance to develop other industrial and agricultural areas. This is a goal that all of the leaders of these nations have clearly in mind.

In Libya, for example, budgets have been steadily increased over the last several years to make agriculture and industry self-supporting; that is, not dependent on oil revenues. The desire to achieve this goal is shared by the other North African nations. Whether this maximum growth rate can be achieved before the oil does run out is by no means certain. But North African leaders agree that it is a race they and their countries cannot afford to lose.

FOR FURTHER READING

Anthony, John. *Tunisia*. New York: Charles Scribner's Sons, 1972.

Ashford, D.E. *Morocco-Tunisia*. Syracuse, N.Y.: Syracuse University Press, 1975.

Brace, R.M. *Morocco, Algeria, Tunisia*. Englewood Cliffs, N.J.: Prentice-Hall Co., 1964.

"Economic Survey." *The New York Times*, February 5, 1978.

Field, Michael, ed. *Middle East Annual Review*. Essex, England: Saffron Walden, 1978. Distributed in the United States and Canada by Rand McNally & Co., Chicago, San Francisco, and New York.

Khadduri, Majed. *Modern Libya*. Baltimore: Johns Hopkins Press, 1973

McKown, Robin. *The Colonial Conquest of Africa*. New York: Franklin Watts, Inc., 1971.

Paxton, John, ed. *The Statesman's Yearbook, 1977-1978*. New York: St. Martin's Press, 1978.

Steel, Ronald, ed. *North Africa, Vol. 38 The Reference Shelf*. New York: H. W. Wilson Co., 1967.

Vlahos, Olivia. *African Beginnings*. New York: The Viking Press, 1967.

INDEX